SOUVENIRS DE *Noël*

....

....

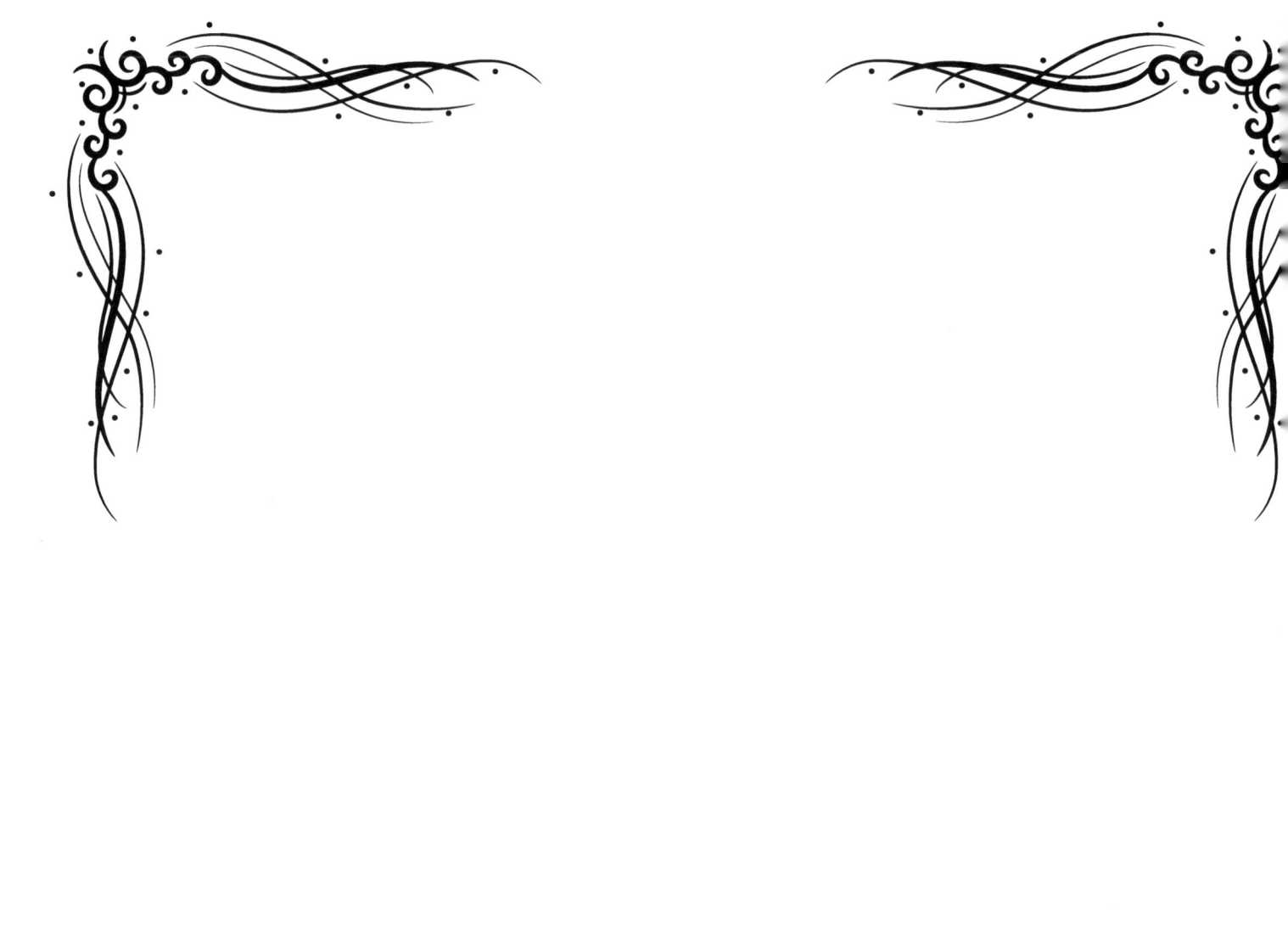

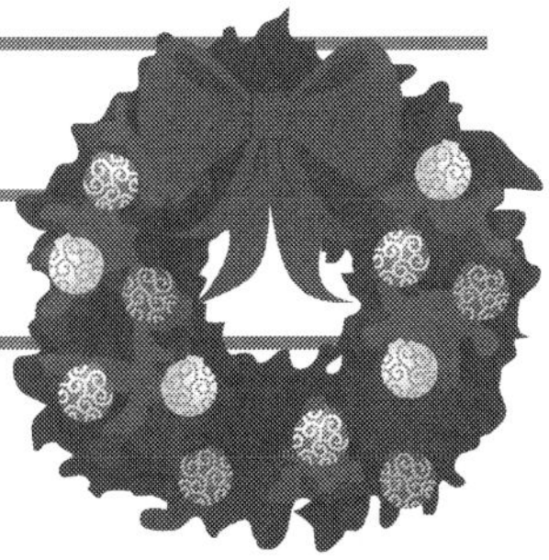

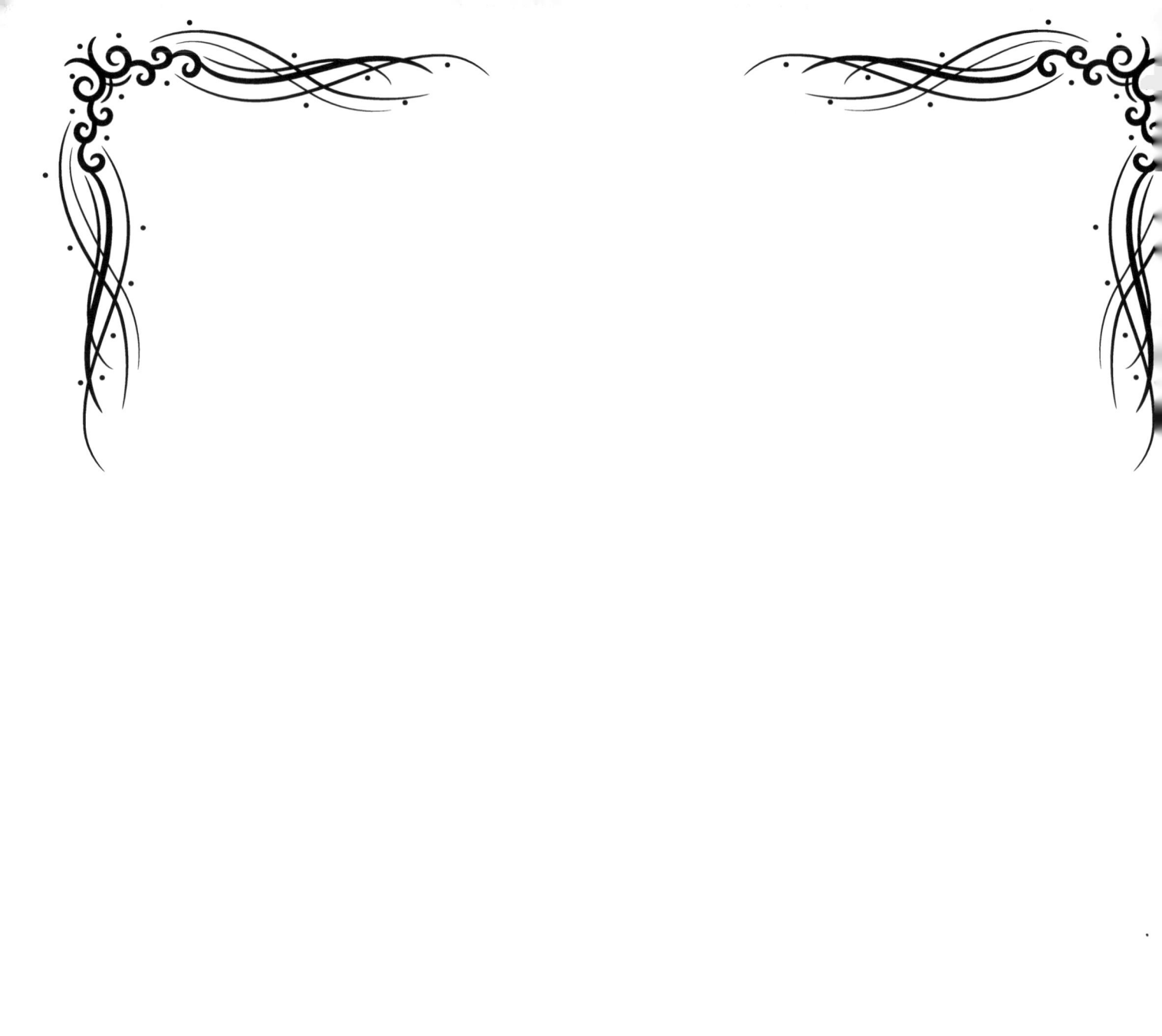

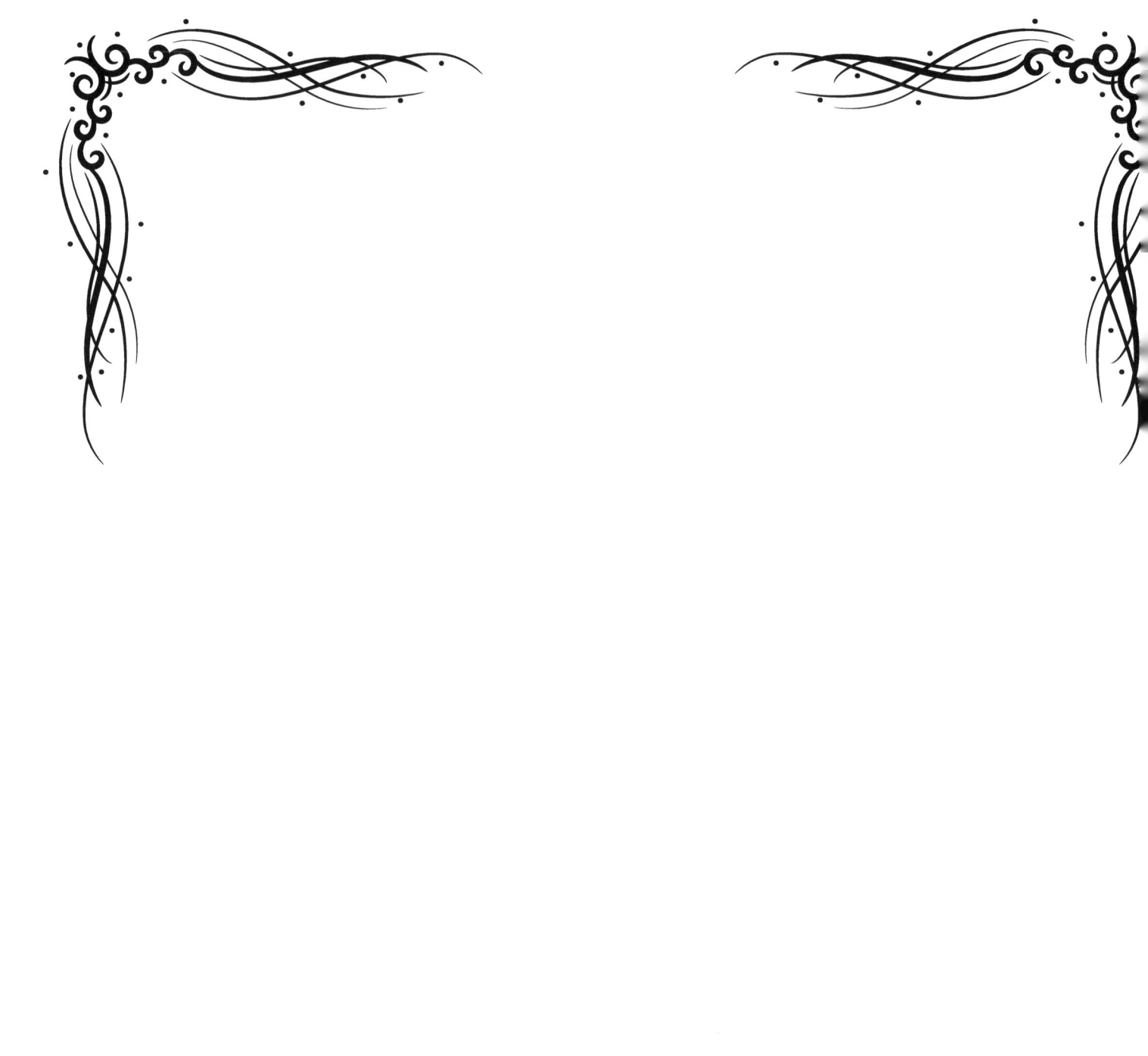

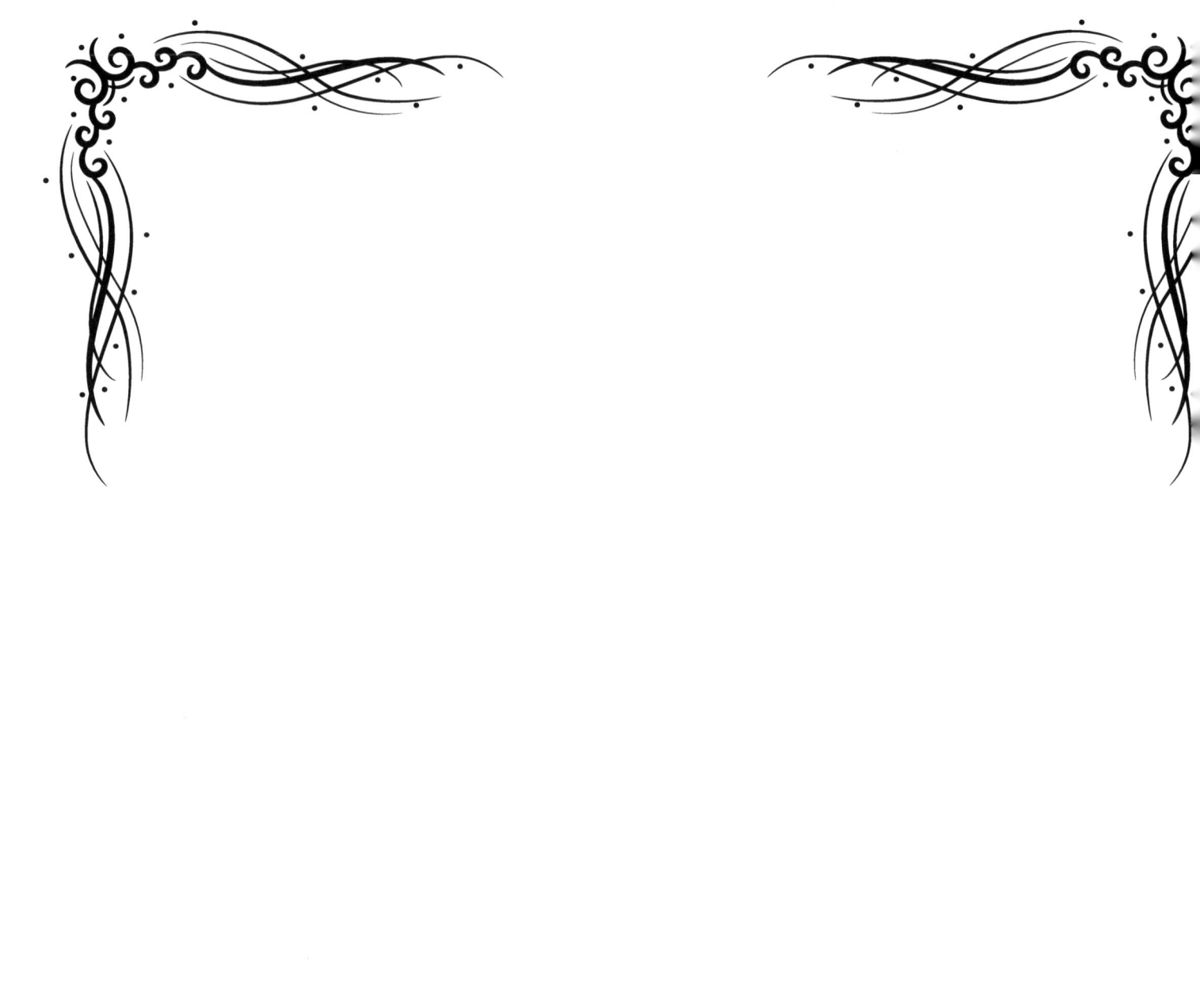

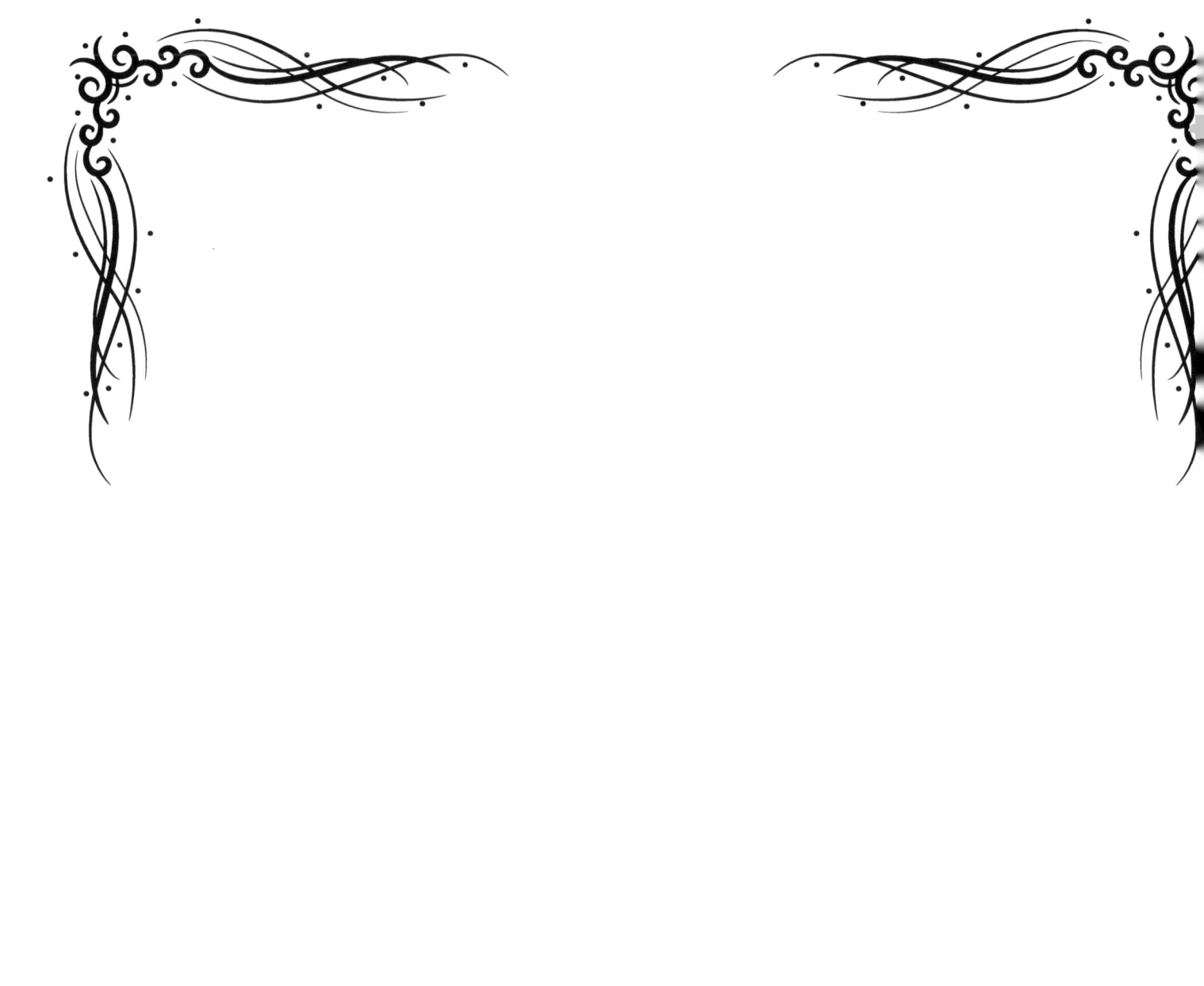

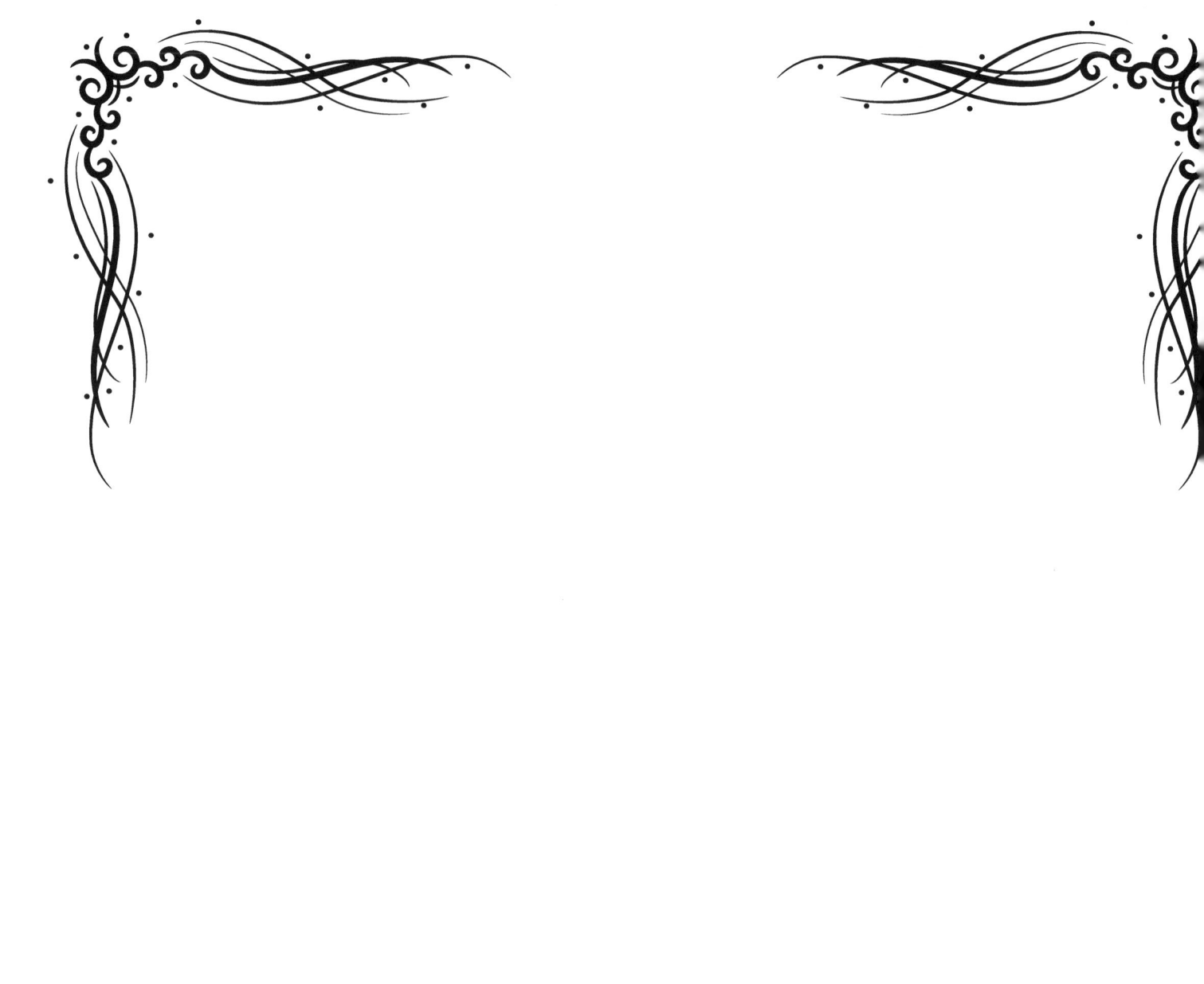

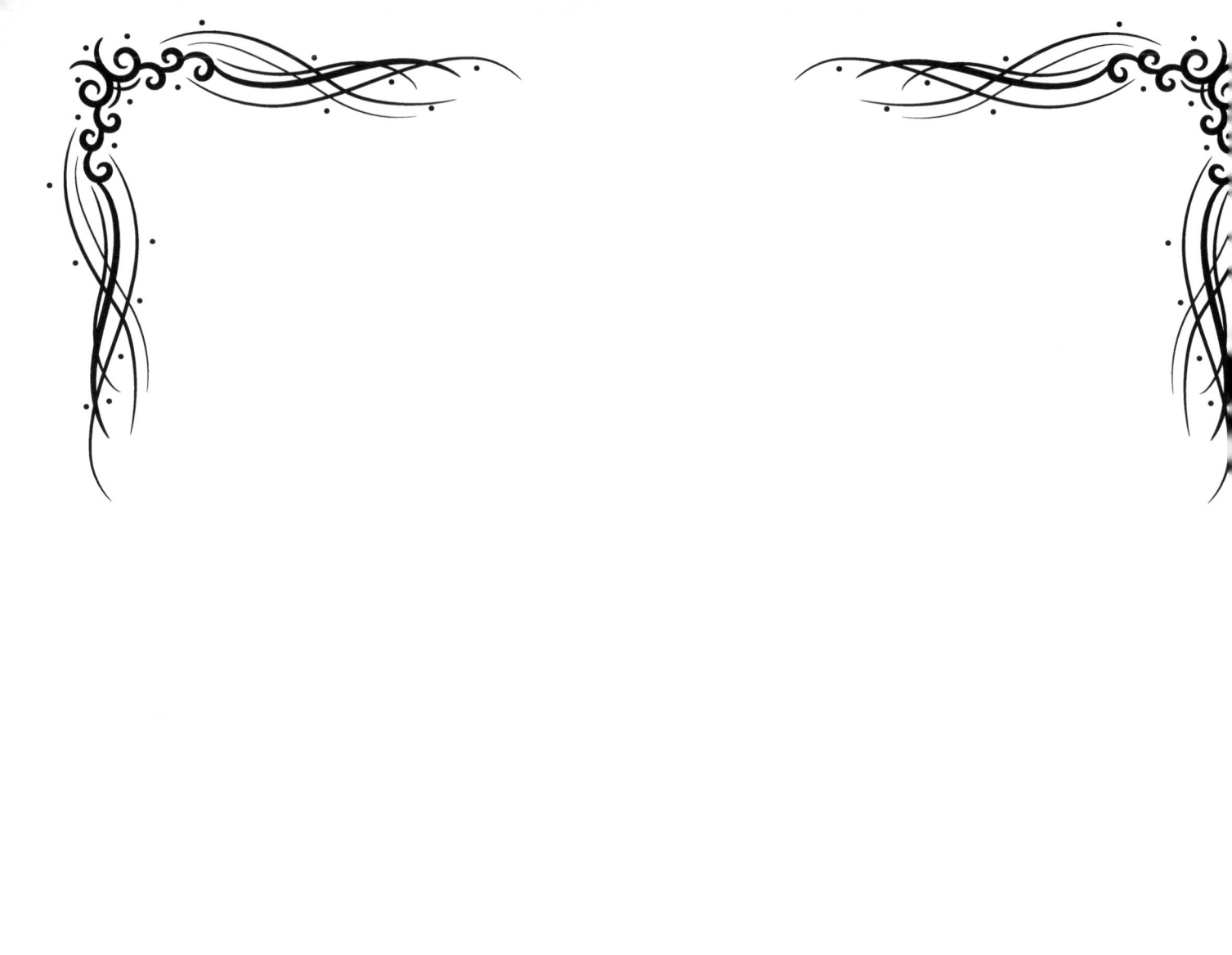

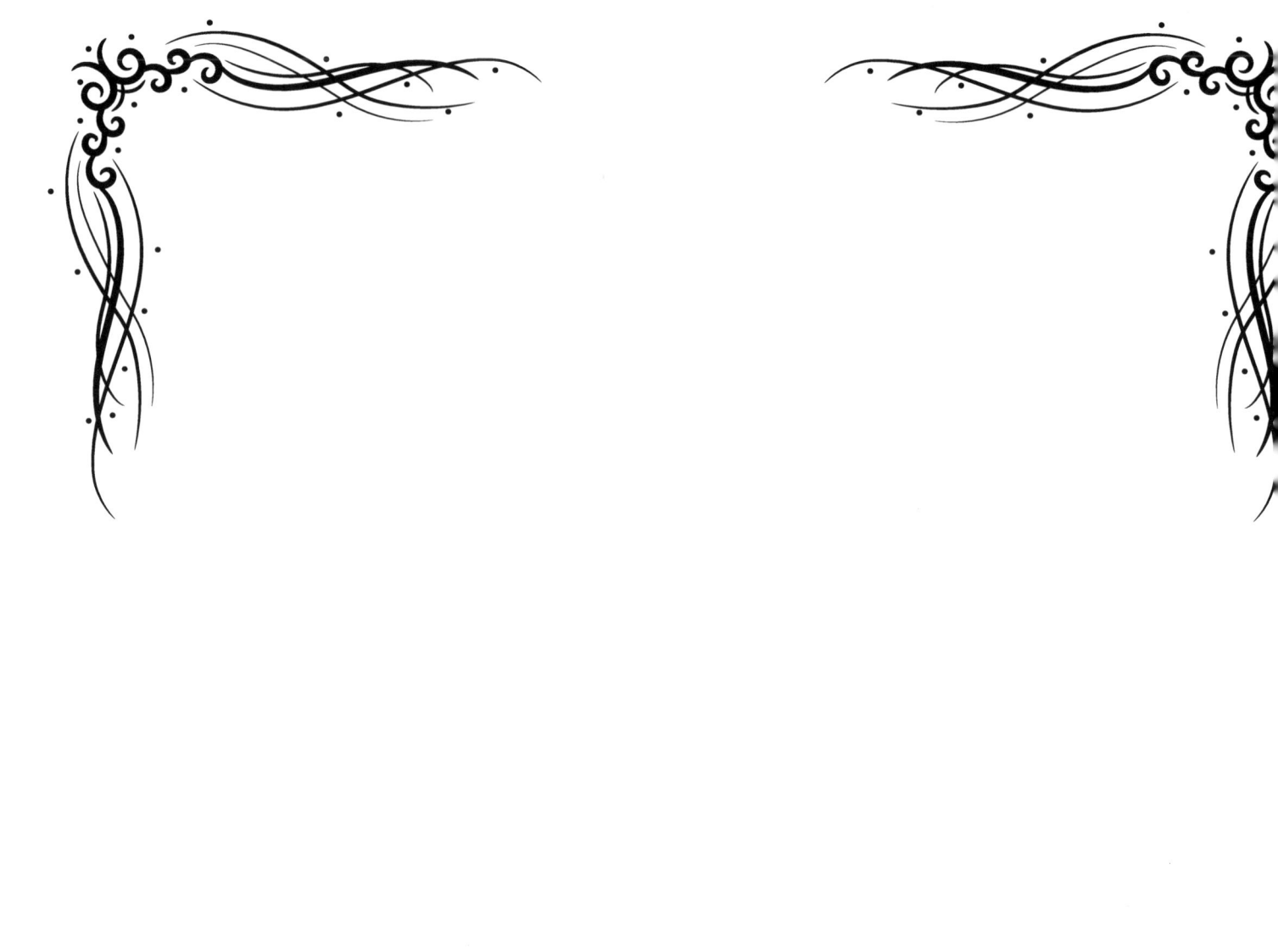

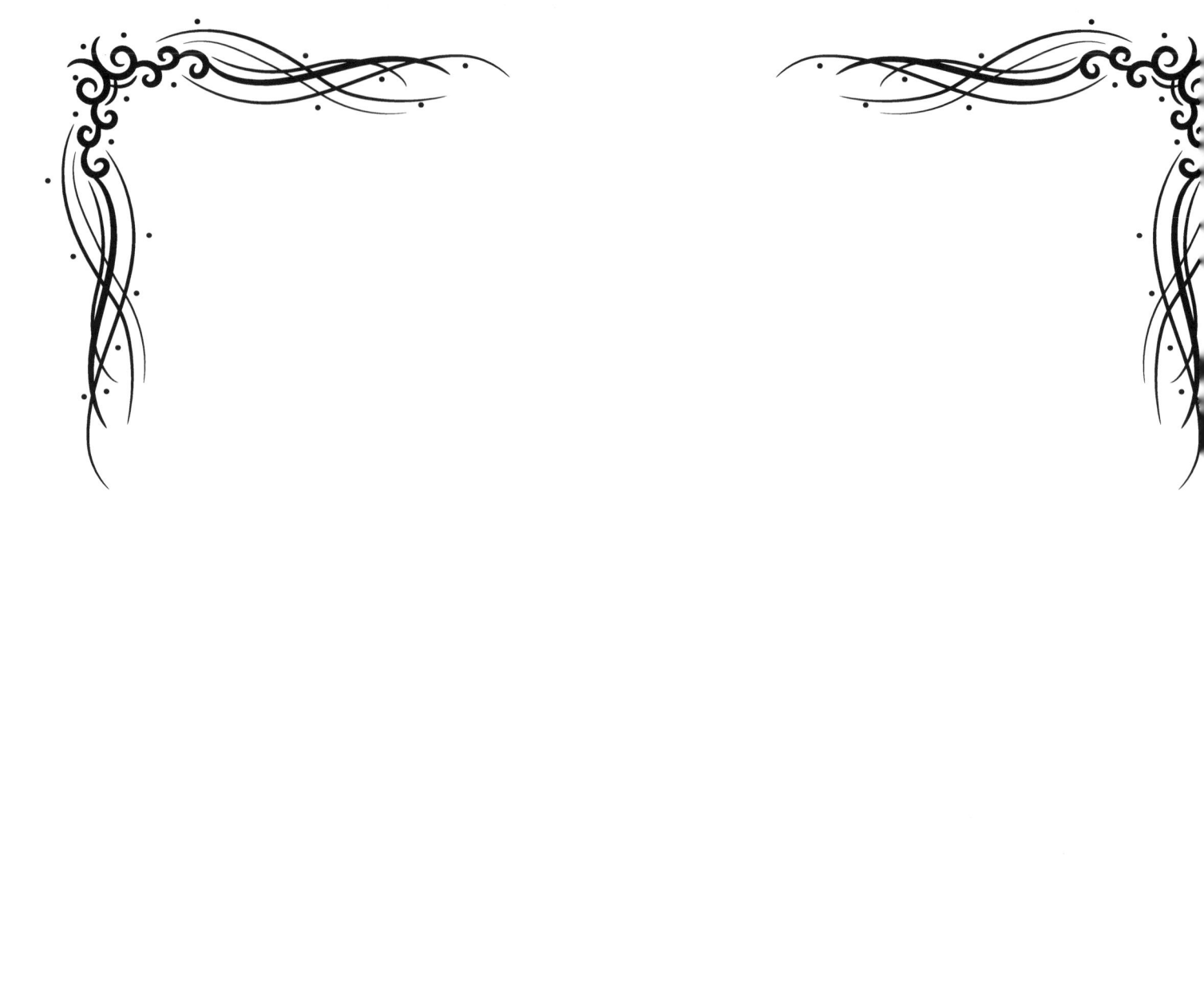

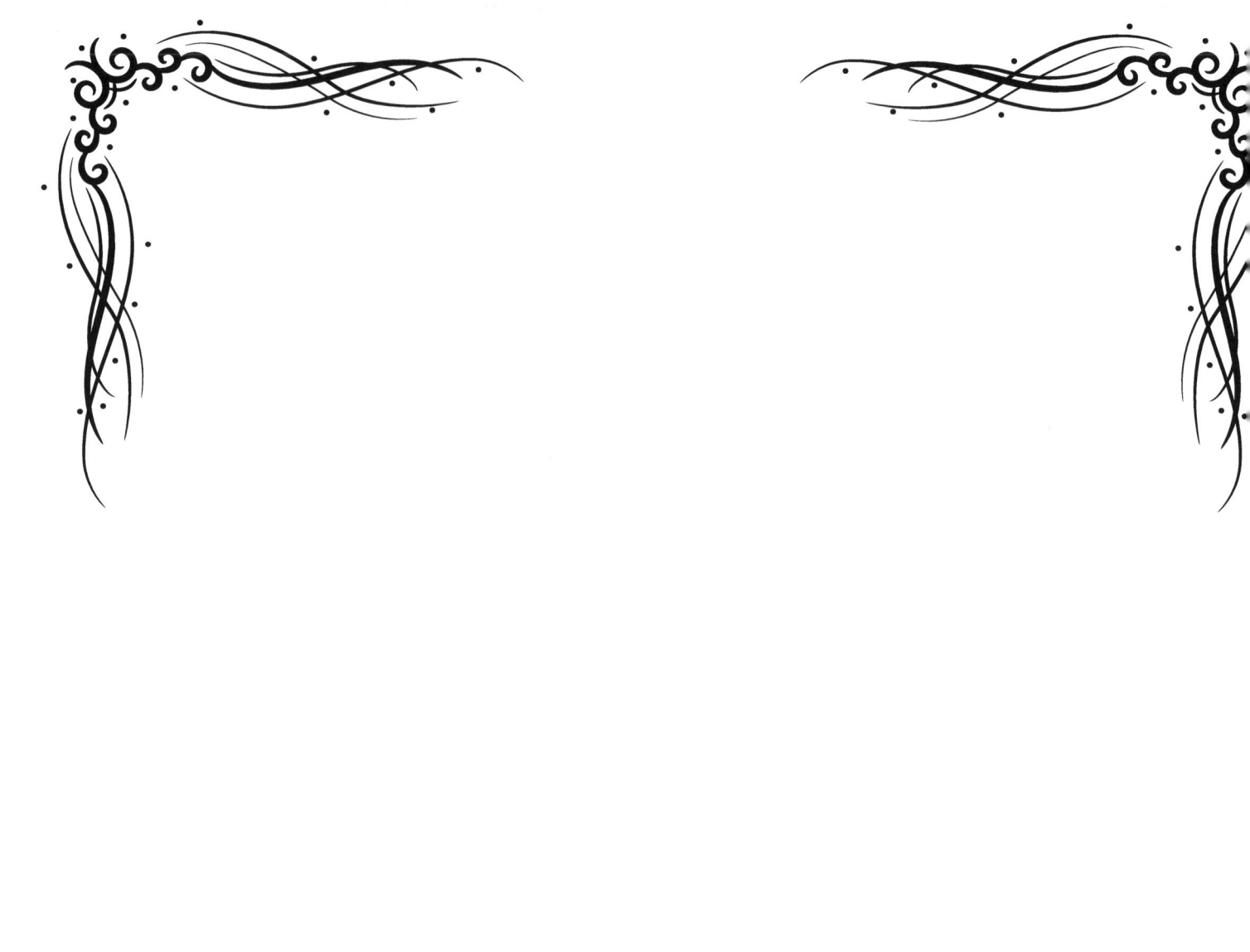

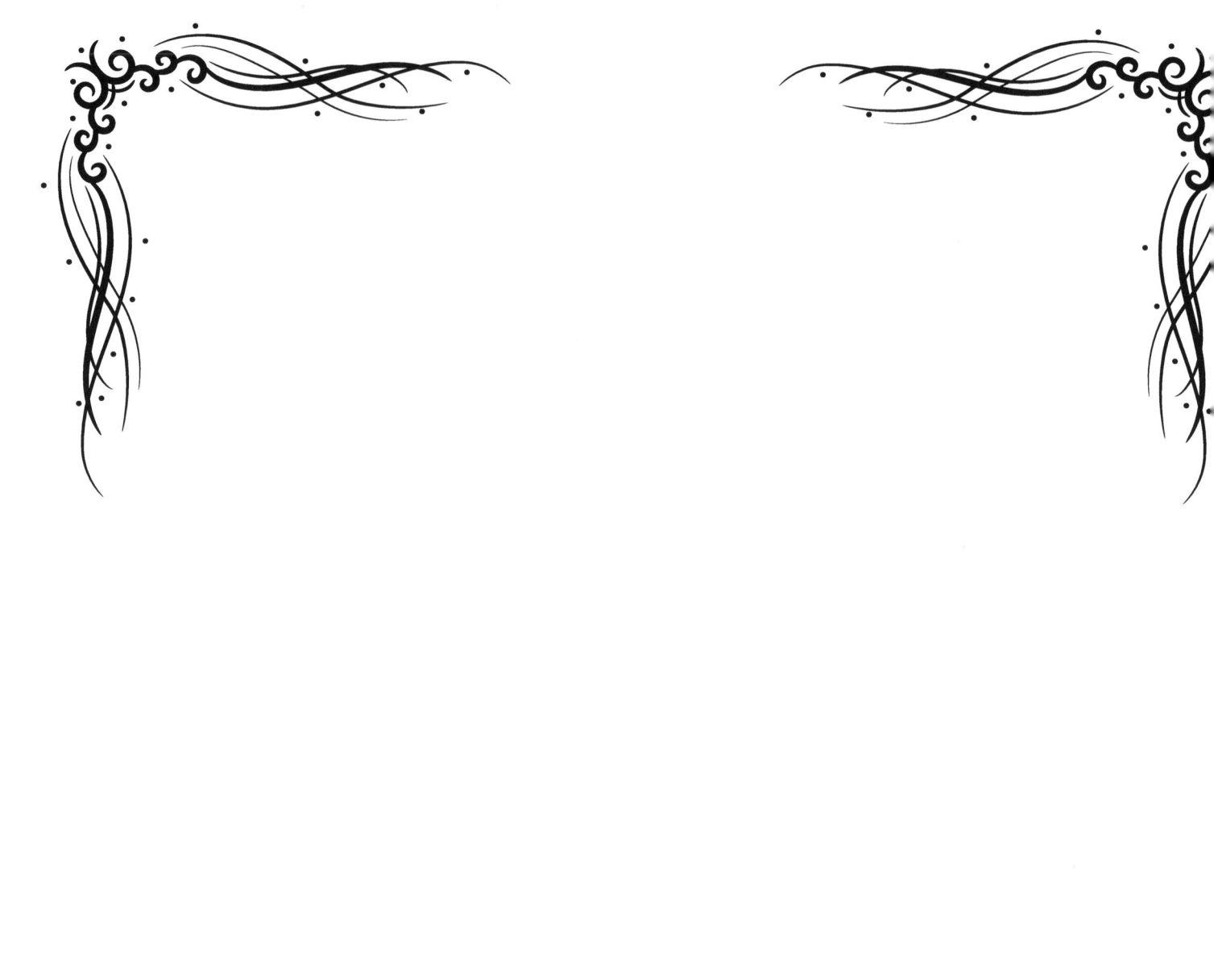

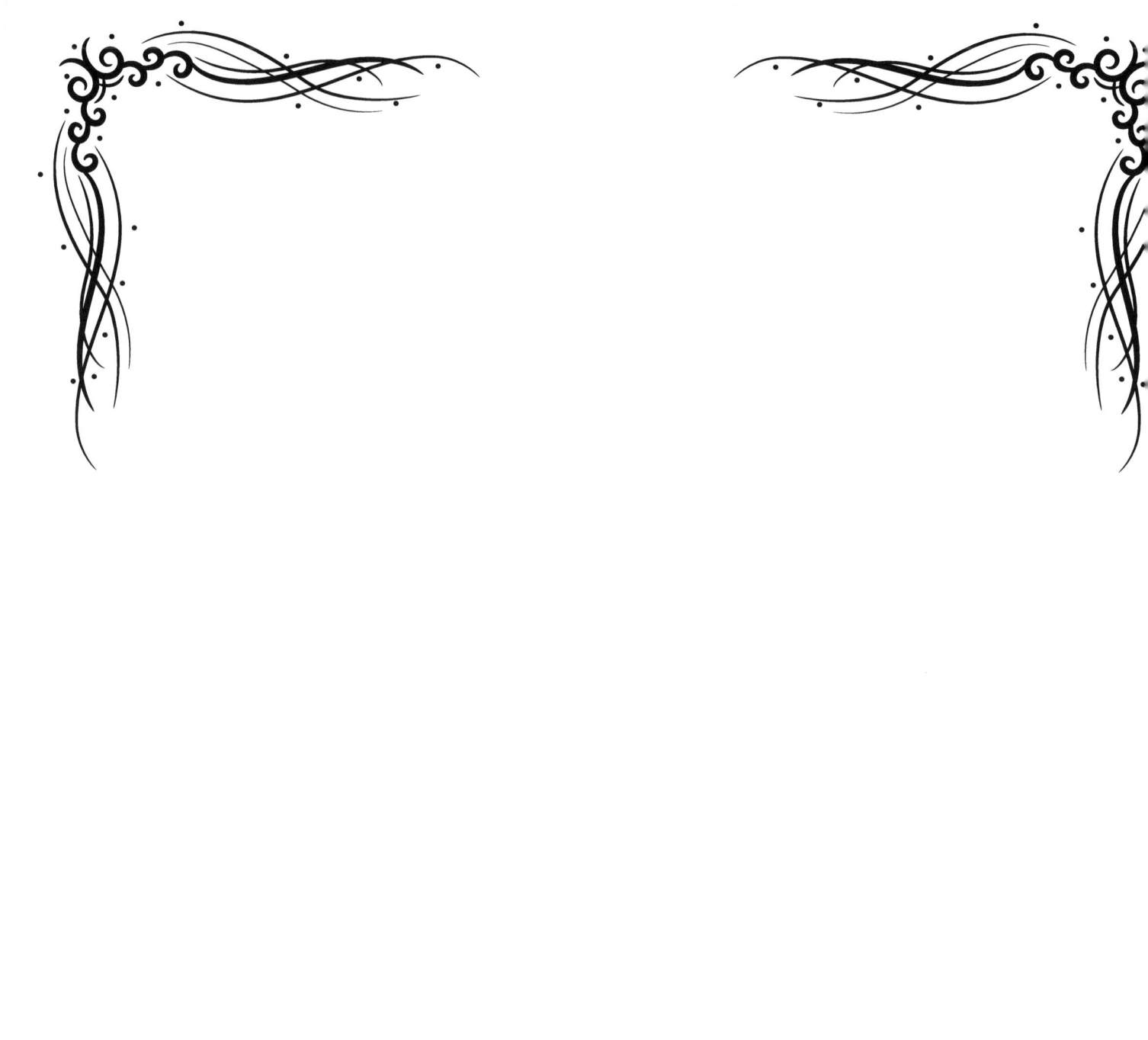

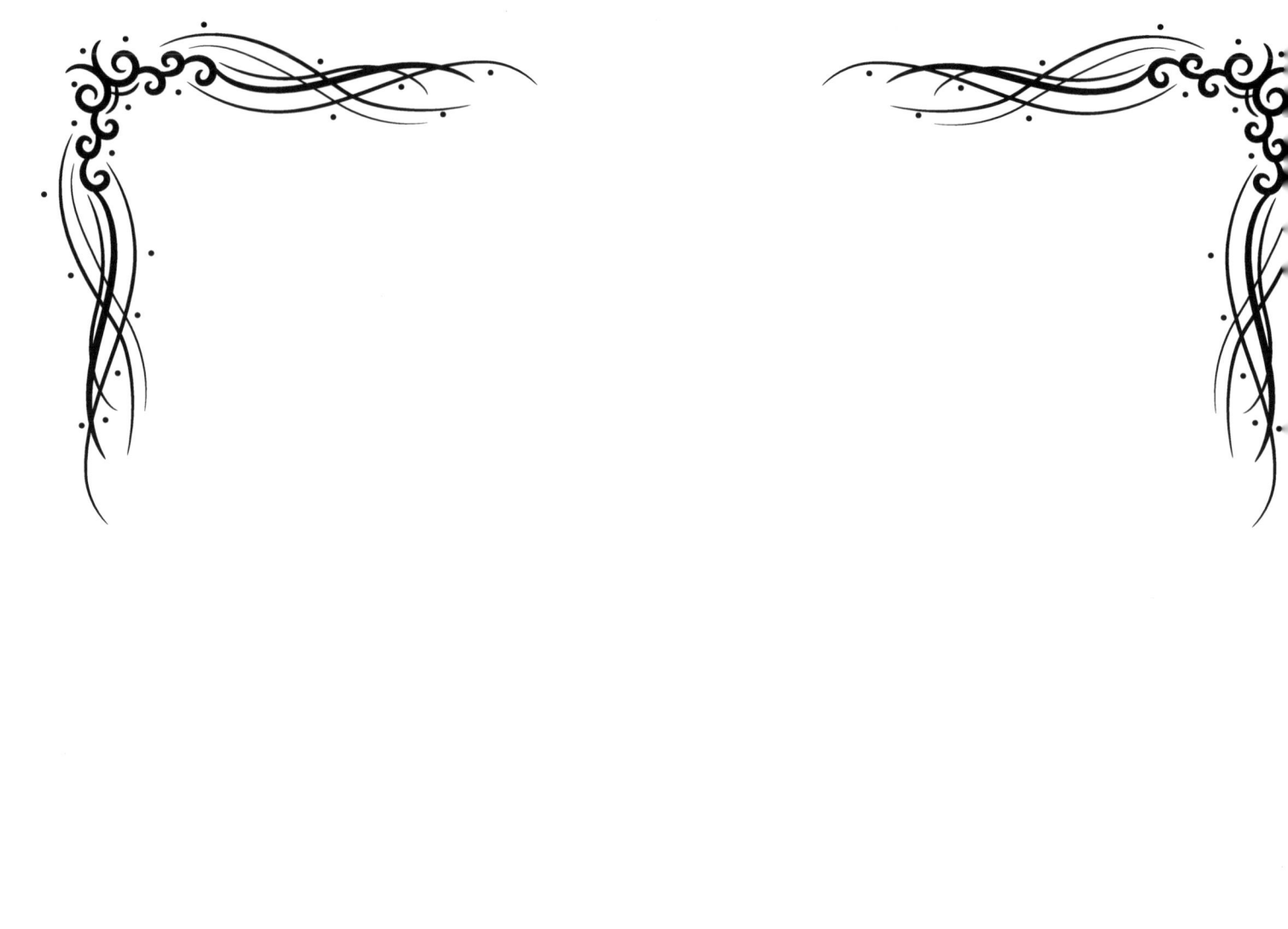

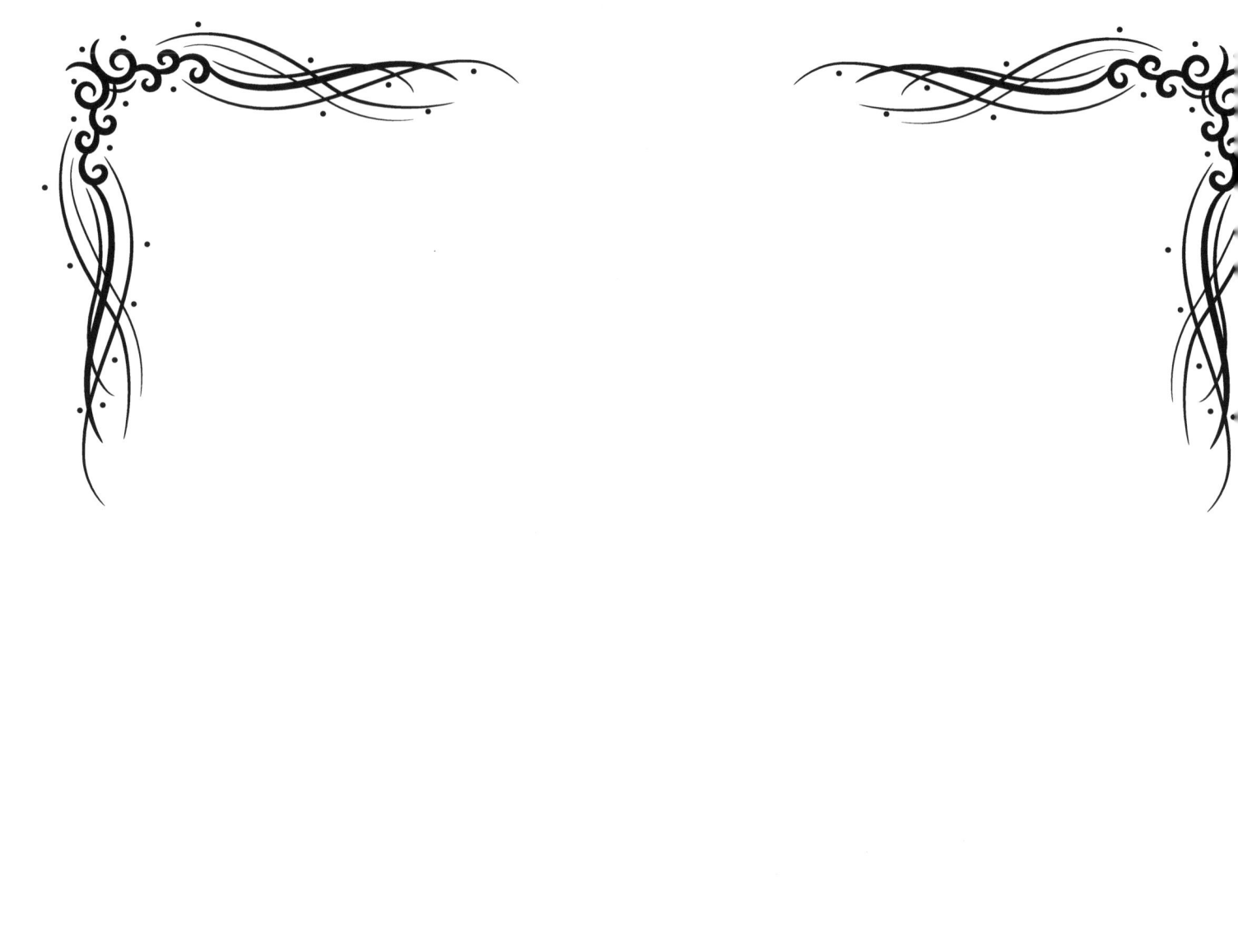

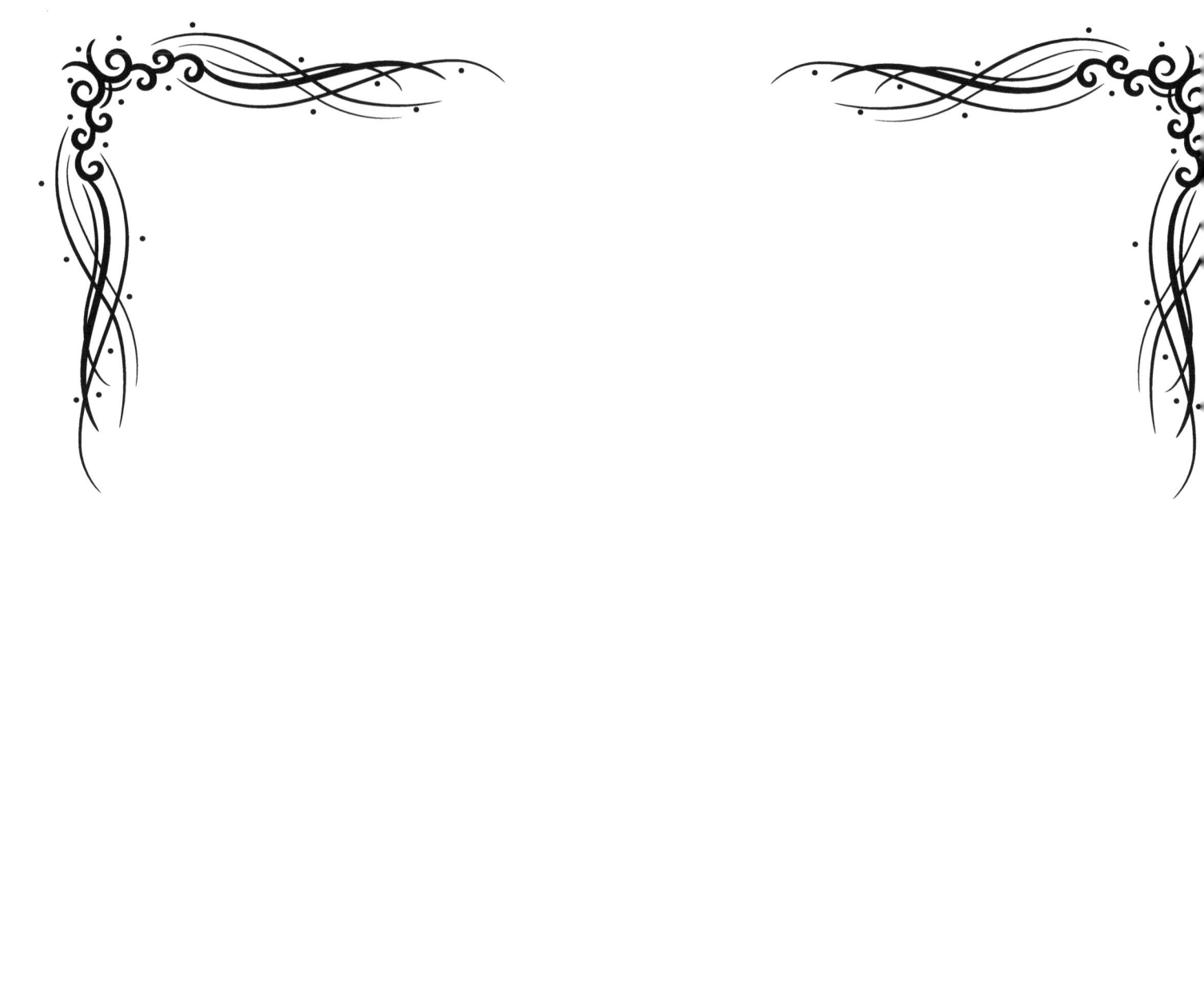

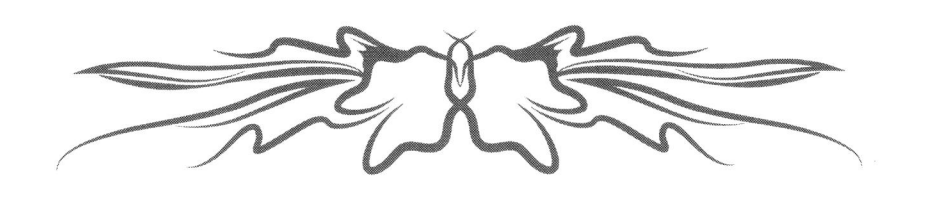

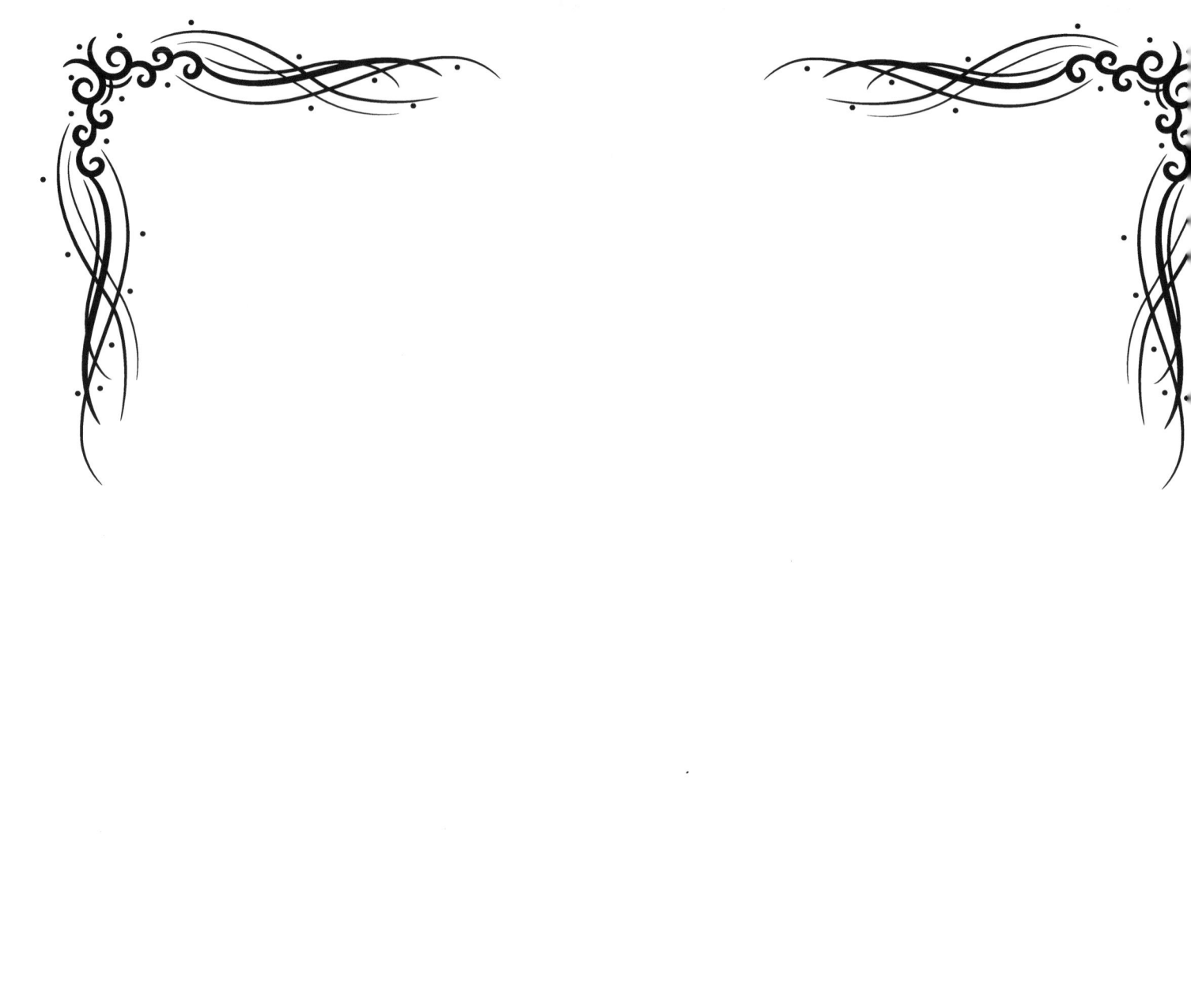

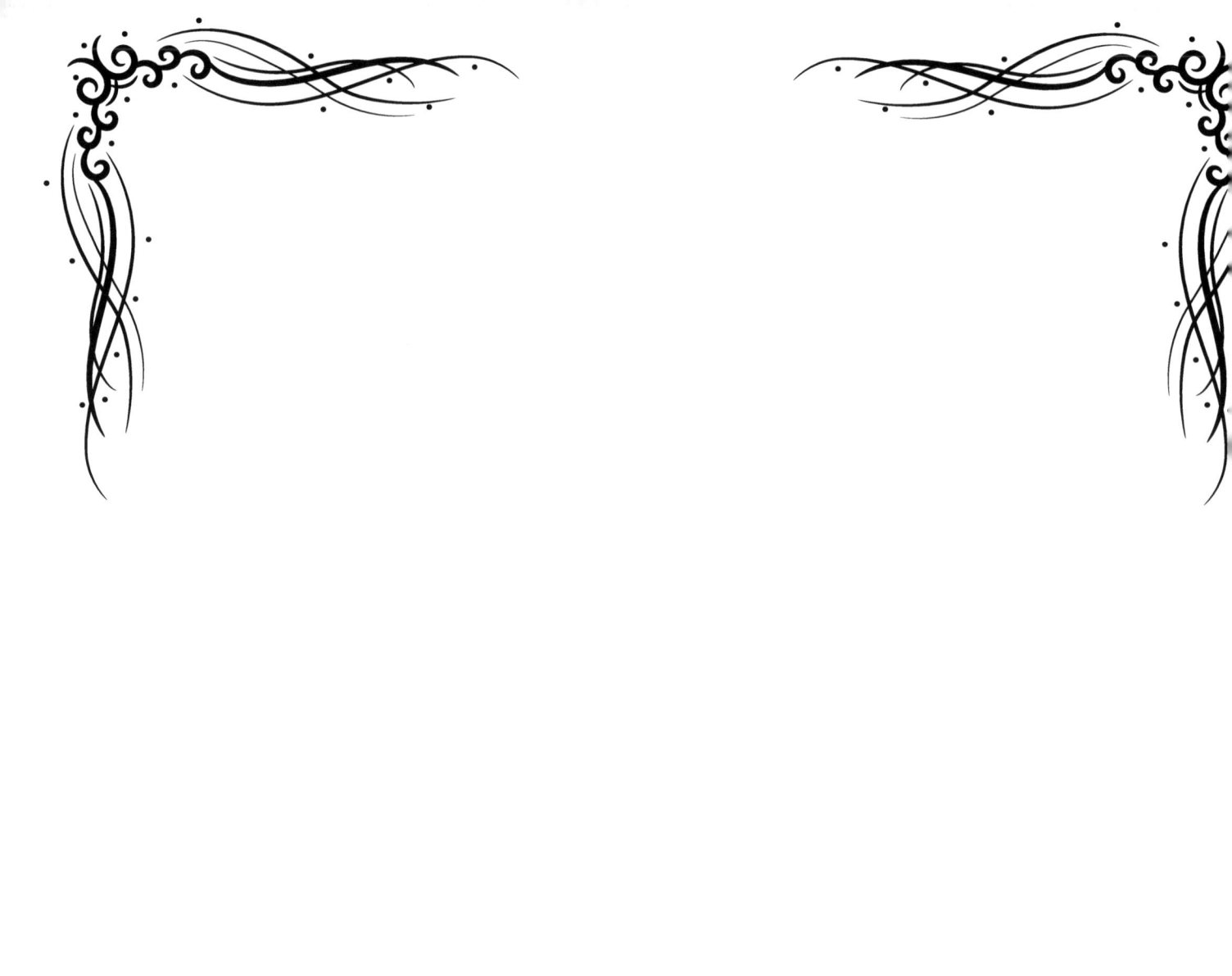

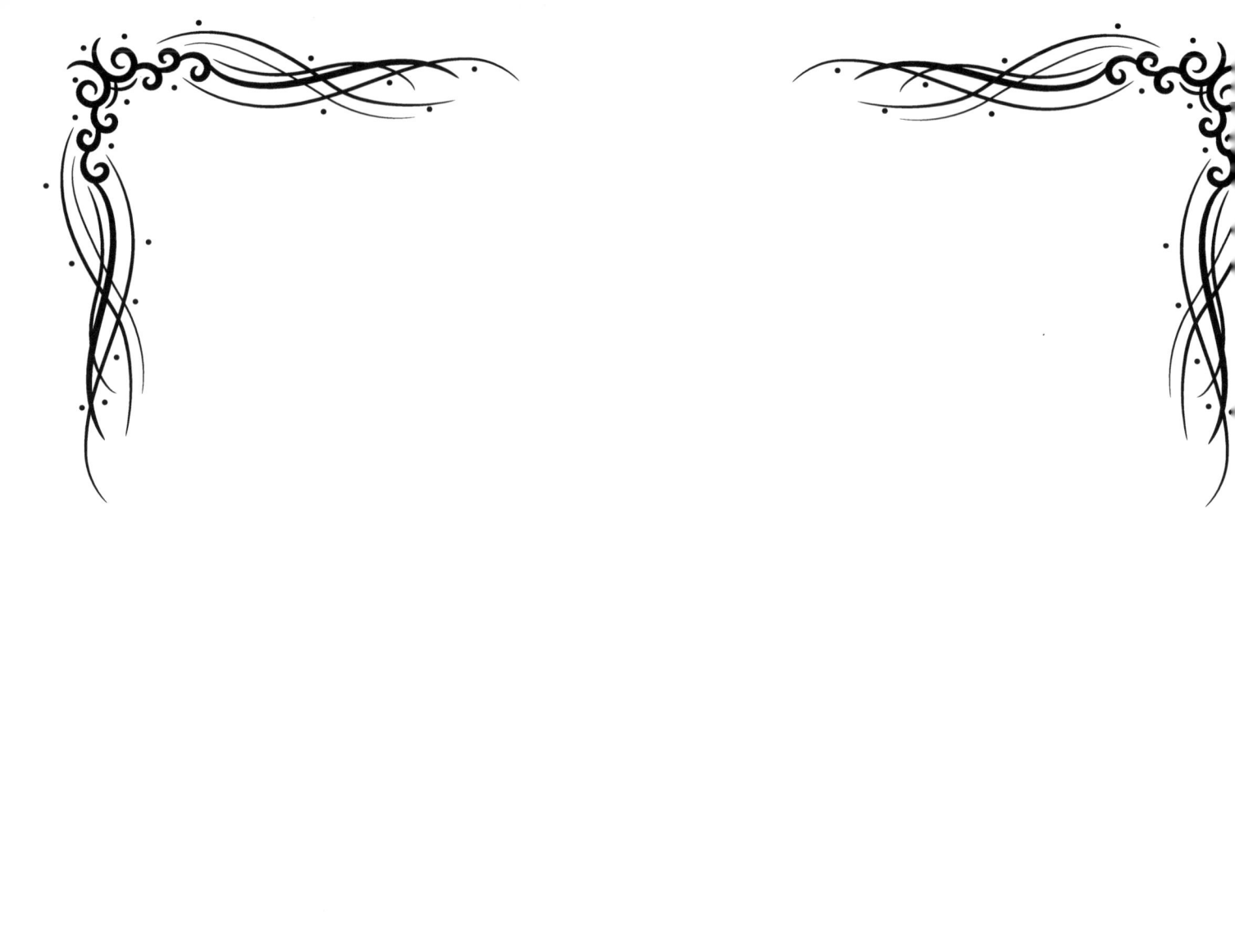

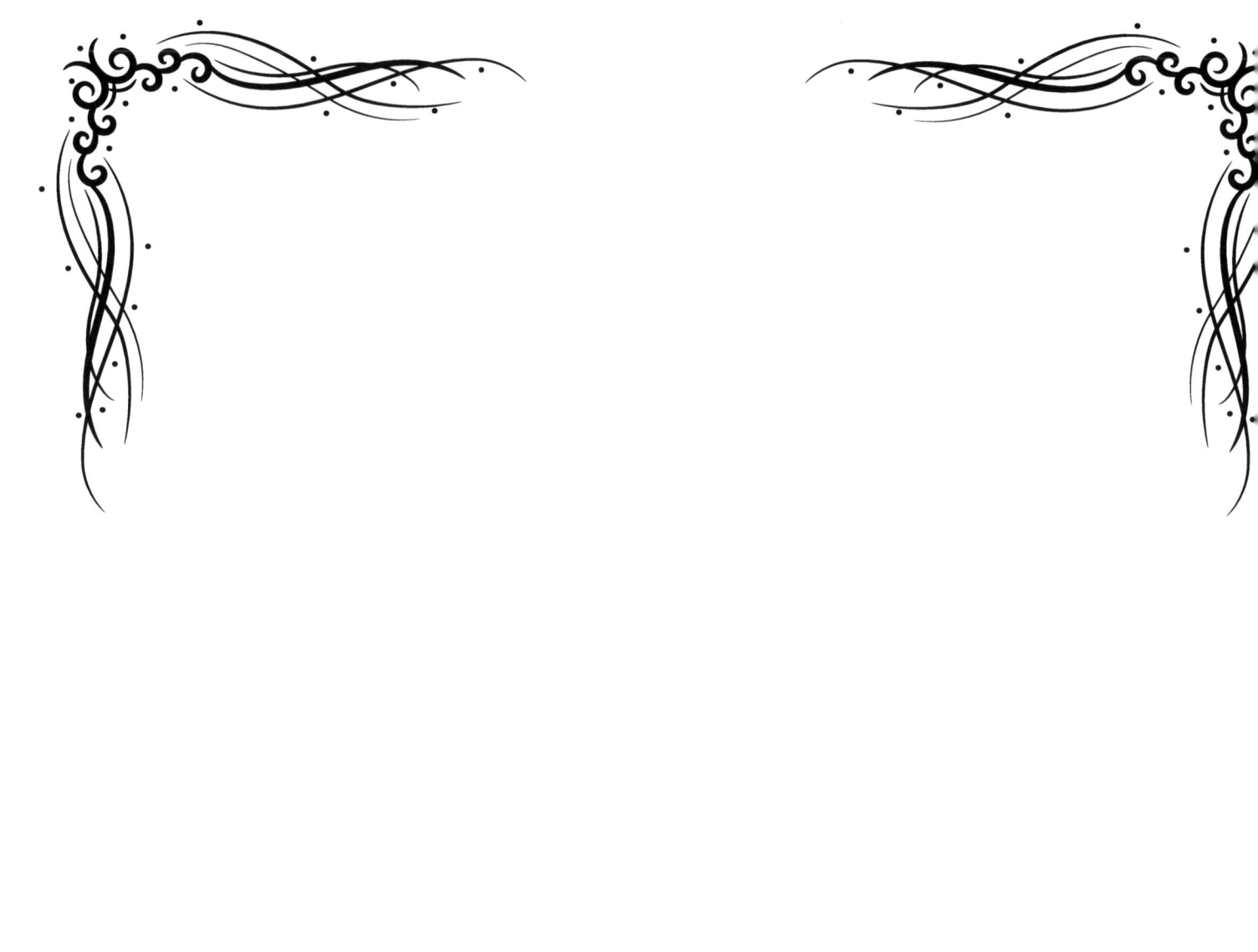

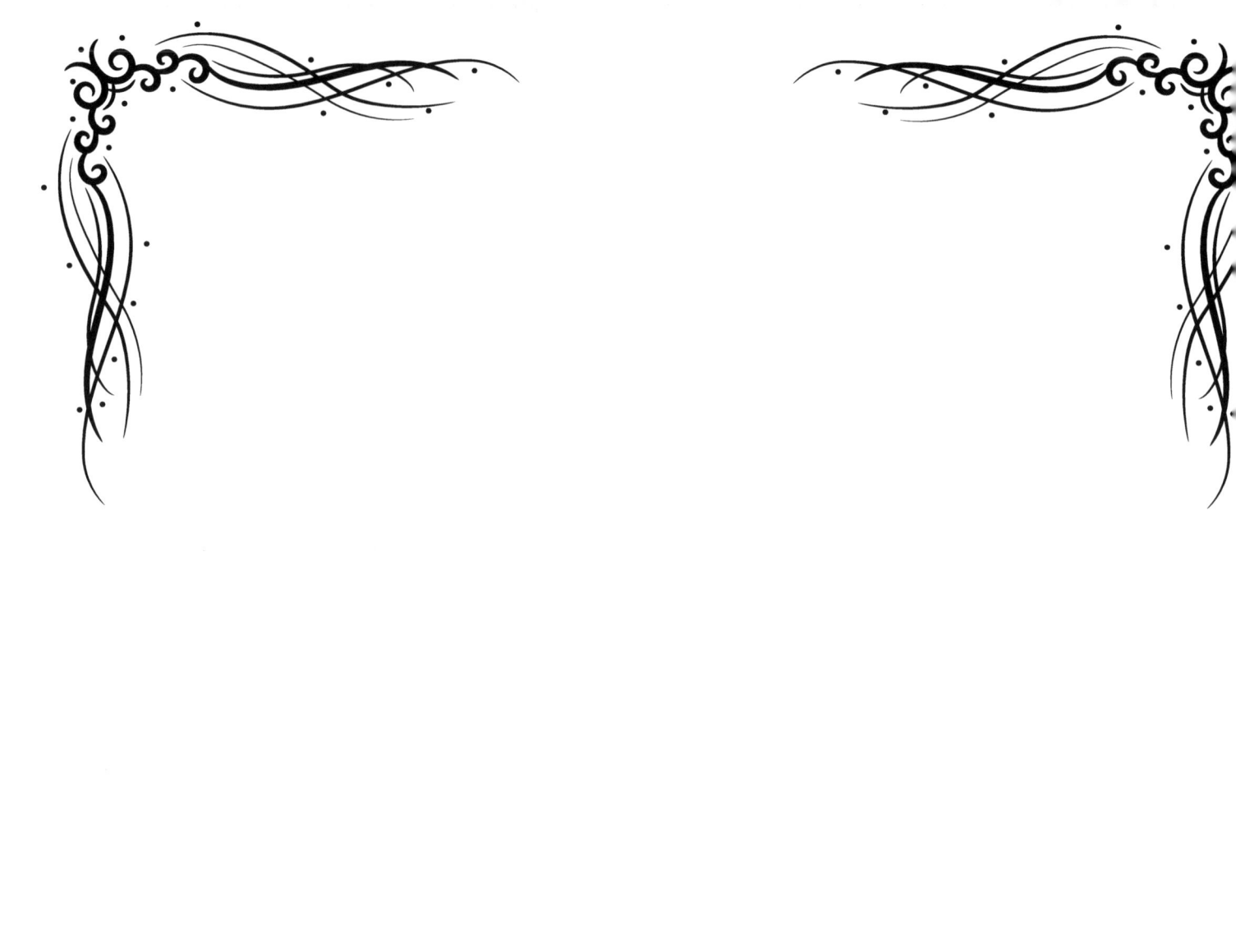

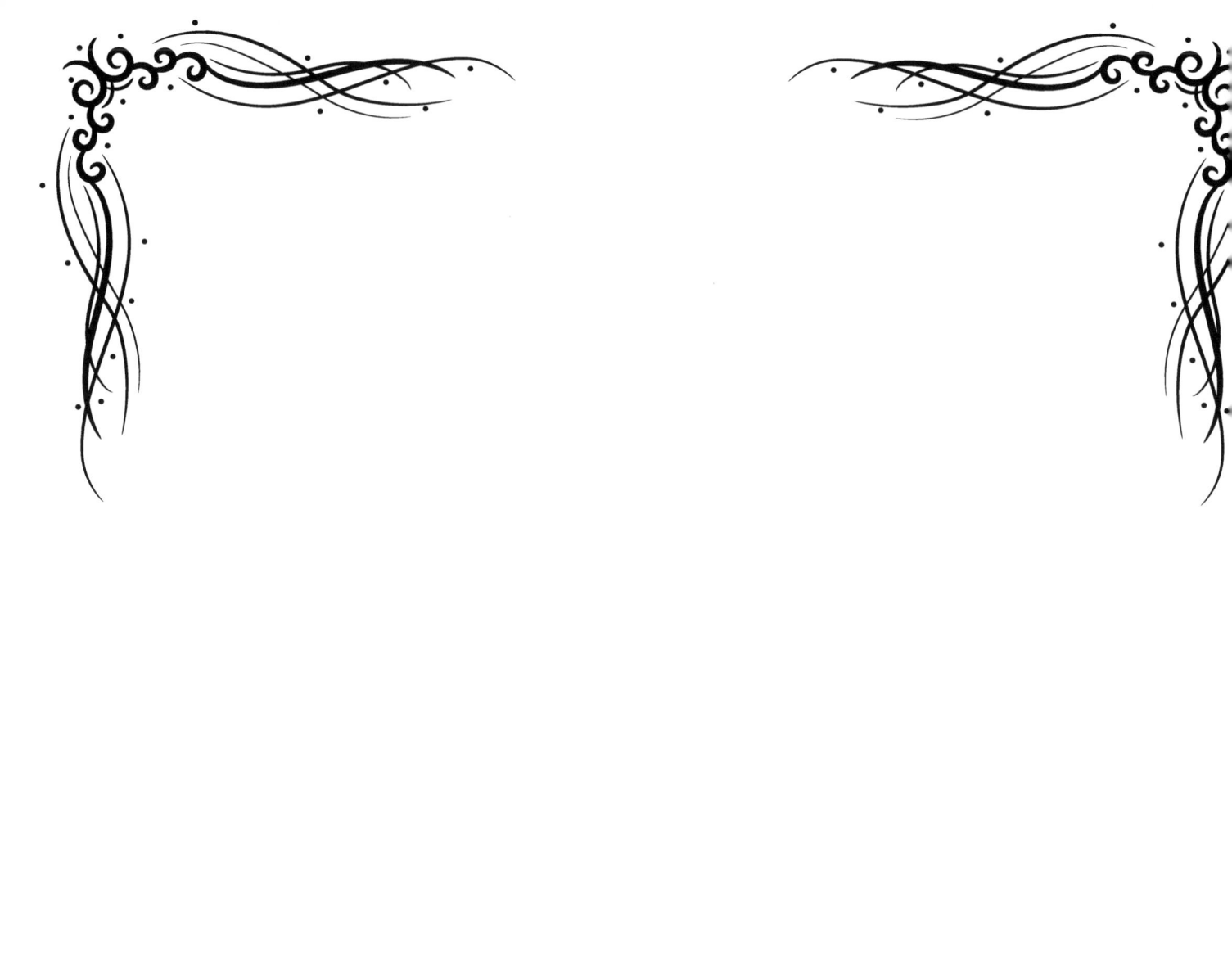

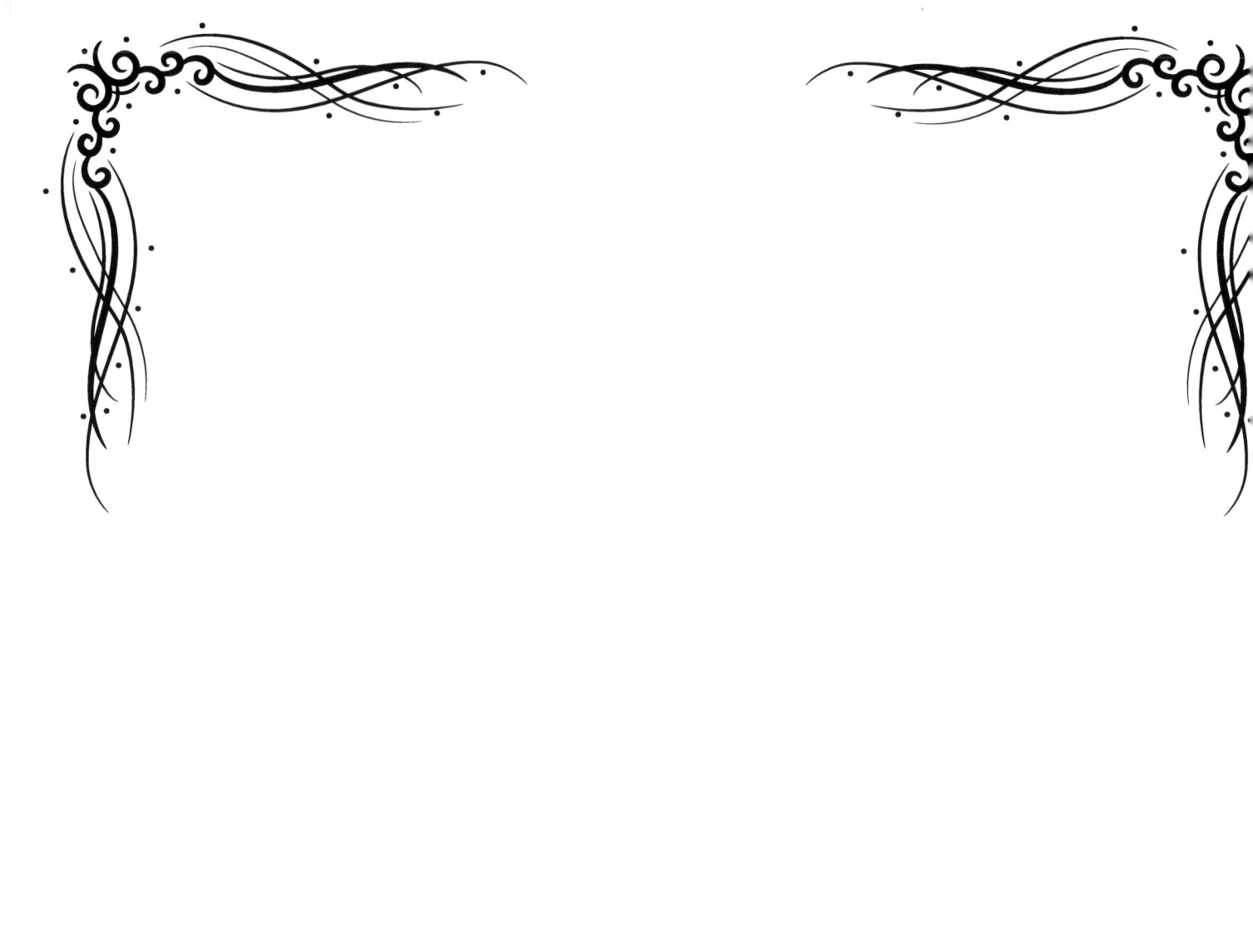

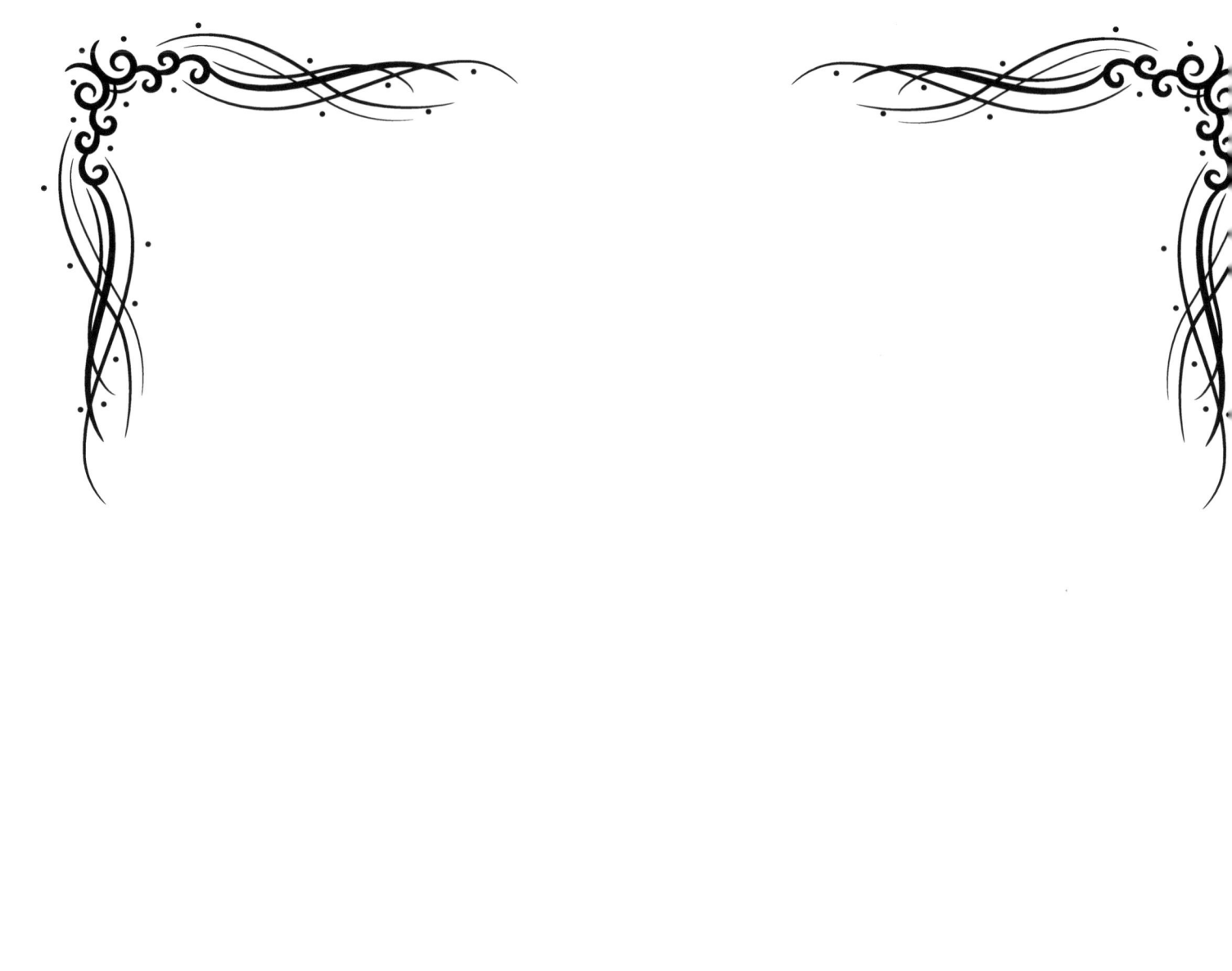

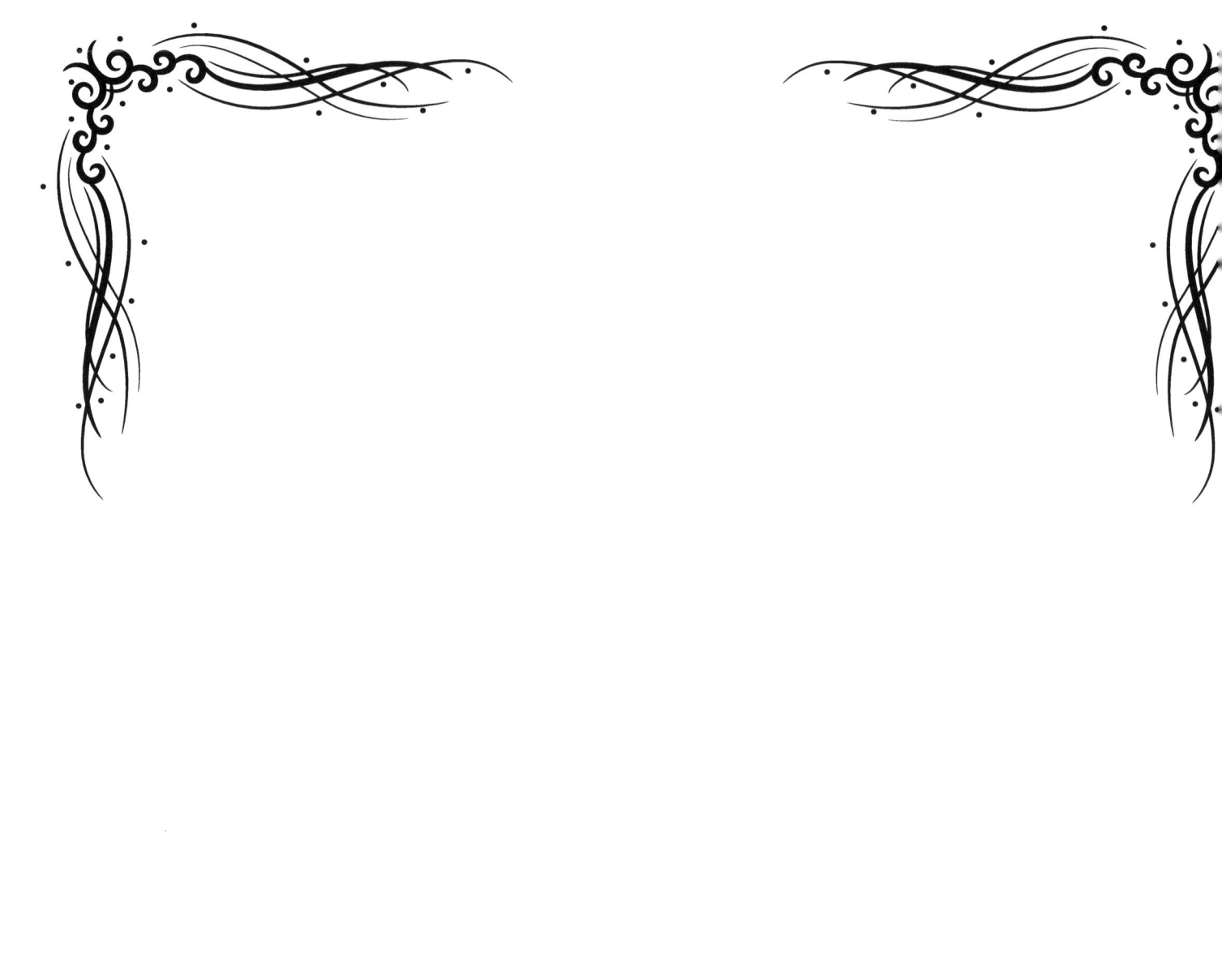

Printed in Great Britain
by Amazon

49293056R00052